I0820419

MISSION: SPACE SCIENCE

Published in 2025 by **Cheriton Children's Books**
1 Bank Drive West, Shrewsbury, Shropshire, SY3 9DJ

First Edition

Author: Sarah Eason
Designers: Paul Myerscough and Steve Mead
Editor: Jennifer Sanderson
Proofreader: Ella Newby
Consultant: David Hawksett, BSc

Picture credits: Cover: Shutterstock/D'Action Images (t), Shutterstock/Lukasz Pawel Szczepanski (b). Inside: p4: Shutterstock/D K Pattanaik, p5: Wikimedia Commons/Simon Wakefield, p6b: Shutterstock/Berna Koritan Sonmez, p6t: Shutterstock/Maradon 333, p7: Shutterstock/Trappy76, p8: Wikimedia Commons/Andreas Cellarius, p9: NASA/SDO/AIA, p10: NASA/JPL/USGS, p11: Wikimedia Commons/Wellcome Collection, p12: NASA/GSFC/SDO, p13: NASA, p14: NASA, p15: Shutterstock/G-Stock Studio, p16: NASA, p17: NASA, p18: Wikimedia Commons/Orren Jack Turner, p19: US Department of Energy, p20: Shutterstock/Olesia Ru, p21: NASA, p22: NASA/Aubrey Gemignani, p23: NASA/SDO/AIA, pp24-25: Shutterstock/Simon's passion 4 Travel, p24t: NASA/GSFC/SDO, p26: NASA/Goddard/SDO, p27: NASA/GSFC/SOHO/ESA, p28: NASA/JPL-Caltech/Harvard-Smithsonian CfA, p29: NASA/JPL-Caltech, p30: NASA/ESA/STScI/G. Bacon, p31: NASA/JPL-Caltech, p32: NASA, p33: Shutterstock/A. Hornung, p34: NASA/Bill Ingalls, p35: Wikimedia Commons/Google Cultural Institute/JgFRcl7gLXKP2Q, p36: NASA/Carla Thomas, p37: NASA/Carla Thomas, p38: NASA/GFSC, p39: NASA/GSFC/SDO, p40: NASA, p41: NASA/JPL-Caltech/NRL/GSFC, p42: NASA/SDO, p43: Flickr/NASA, p44: Wikimedia Commons/NASA/Johns Hopkins APL/Steve Gribben, p45: Shutterstock/Gorodenkoff.

Printed in China

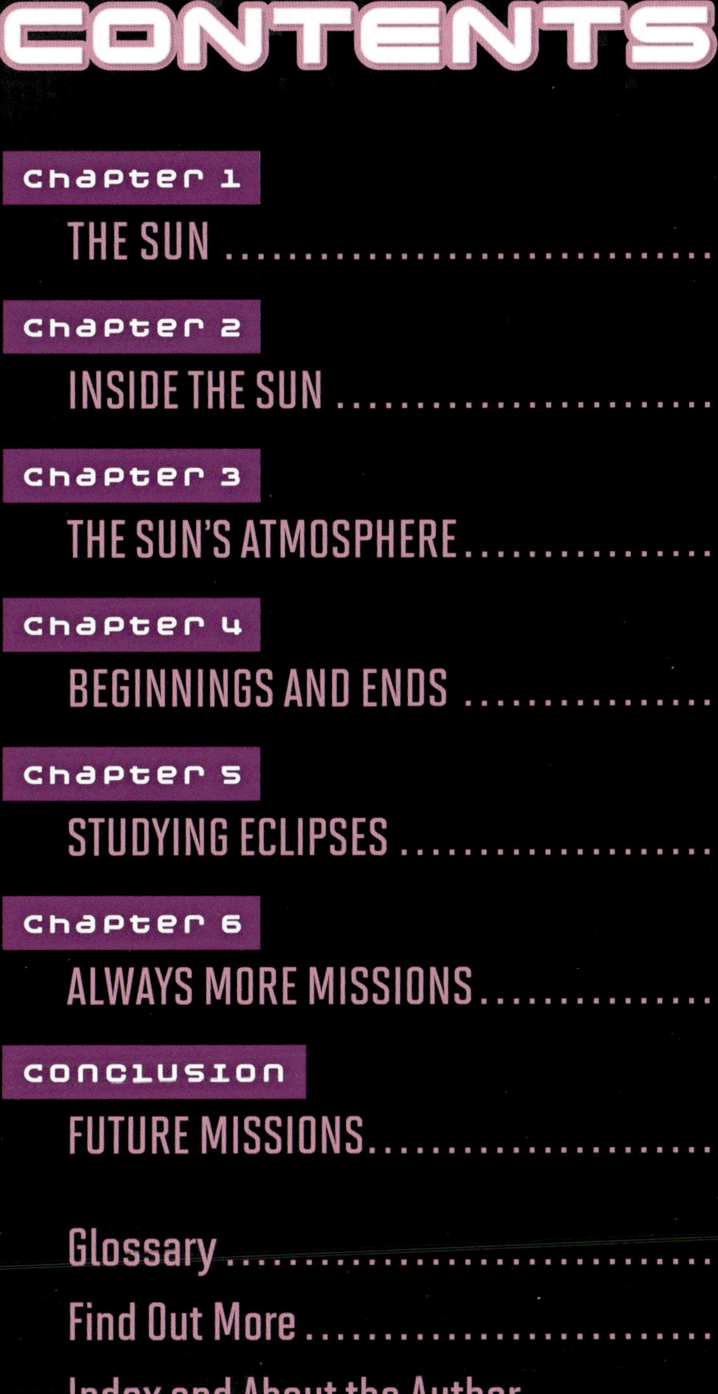

CONTENTS

Chapter 1

THE SUN

From the tiniest bacteria to the tallest trees, almost all life on Earth depends on the sun. Humans need its light to see, its heat to keep us warm, and both to support life. The sun is incredibly important to us, but it is not unique. It is just one of billions of similar, medium-sized stars found in our galaxy and elsewhere in the universe. However, for most of human history, people did not realize this. Instead, the sun was seen by many as like a god.

The Sun God Ra

For the ancient Egyptians, the sun represented light, warmth, and growth, and was depicted by Ra, one of their most important gods. Ra was believed to have created all forms of life by calling their secret names. However, the sun god could be a destroyer as well as a creator. In one story he became angry with humans and sent his eye, in the form of the lion-headed goddess Sekhmet, to punish them.

Another Sun God

In Hinduism, Surya is the sun god. His sons include the first man on Earth, the lord of death, a great warrior, and king of the monkeys. Surya had the power of banishing darkness and curing disease.

Surya is the Hindu god of the sun. He is believed to be the creator of the universe and the source of all life.

Ancient people in Britain may have used Stonehenge to help them monitor time using the position of the sun in the sky (see below).

A Chariot-Driving God

The ancient Greeks saw the sun as a god called Helios, who drove the sun across the sky each day in a chariot pulled by flying horses. This was their way of explaining why the sun moves from east to west each day. Other cultures have similar myths serving the same purpose. For example, Norse myths tell of the horses Arvakr and Alsvid, who pull the sun's chariot.

Space History

Even thousands of years ago, people could accurately track the sun's position as it changed throughout the year, and many ancient structures were built to match the sun's position in the sky. For example, the stones at Stonehenge in England are aligned to frame the sun during the summer and winter solstices. The Mayan pyramid of El Castillo is designed so that serpent-shaped shadows appear to slither down its sides during the spring and fall equinoxes.

Your Mission

In this book we will explore the sun in detail, looking at what we know about them and how we learned it. You will also be given thought-provoking space missions to complete that will draw on:

- Your STEM skills: these are science, technology, engineering, and math skills.
- Your social skills: these include identifying skills and strengths in others, team building, persuasive skills, and learning how to work collaboratively.
- Your critical thinking skills: these include being able to evaluate and analyze information, think independently about problems and find solutions, and draw your own conclusions.

All the above skills are vital for space exploration—ask any space scientist! So, are you mission-ready? Let's begin the missions and find out.

Science and the Sun

The sun was important in religion, but some ancient astronomers studied the sky in a more scientific way. For example, more than 2,000 years ago, Babylonian astronomers were able to trace the path of the sun along the ecliptic over the course of a year. The ecliptic is an imaginary line in the sky that marks the annual path of the sun. The Babylonians were able to see that at some points the sun seemed to slow down or speed up, though they were not able to tell why.

In the Middle Ages, a device called an astrolabe (shown above) was used to make astronomical calculations.

Figured Out with Math

A lot of astronomy depends on mathematical calculations, and the Greek mathematician Eratosthenes (c. 276–c. 194 BCE) made a number of discoveries. He was the first person to calculate the circumference of Earth, and his figure was fairly accurate. He may have calculated the distance from Earth to the sun, too. Not all scientists agree on the translation of his Greek writings, but one version is incredibly accurate. Hundreds of years later, the Greek astronomer Ptolemy (c. 100–c. 170 CE) estimated his own figure of Earth's circumference, which was way off.

Eratosthenes' measurement of Earth's circumference was 0.5 to 17 percent out from modern figures, but it was still in the right range.

Great Arabian Astronomers

Between about 700 and 1500 CE, the Arabic world had its own great astronomers. They studied the stars, and many of them (such as Betelgeuse and Aldebaran) are still known by their Arabic names. They used tools such as astrolabes and armillary spheres to observe and measure the positions of the sun, planets, and stars. For example, the Egyptian astronomer Ibn Yunus (c. 950–c. 1009 CE) recorded more than 10,000 entries of the sun's position over a period of many years. Other Arabian astronomers noticed that the points where the sun's orbit seems to slow down changed over time.

The Aztecs lived in Central America between 1300 and 1521 BCE. They were great astronomers who studied the movement of the sun and planets. They created a stone calendar with the sun at its center to help them chart the seasons.

Space History

The Greek philosopher Anaxagoras (c. 500–c. 428 BCE) was determined to find out how the world worked. He believed that everything followed natural laws. He was one of the first people to suggest that the moon reflects light from the sun, which is true. However, he was wrong about other things. He thought the sun was a mass of blazing metal the size of the Peloponnese, which is a large peninsula in Greece.

At the Center of Everything

Although the sun was recognized in ancient times as being crucial for life on Earth, most people believed Earth was the center of everything. Our home planet stayed in one position, they thought, and everything else traveled in circles around it. The sun rose in the east and moved across the sky to set in the west, and ancient people believed that was because the sun was traveling around Earth, and not the other way around. It naturally followed, then, that everything else revolved around Earth, too.

A Model Solar System

Ptolemy figured out a model to show how the solar system worked. His version had the moon orbiting closest to Earth, followed by Mercury and Venus, then the sun. After that were the other known planets in the correct order. However, although on the surface this seemed to work, the mathematics of the theory did not quite match up with people's observations of the night sky.

The burning ball of gas that is our sun has fascinated astronomers for centuries. However, scientists had different theories about its position in the solar system.

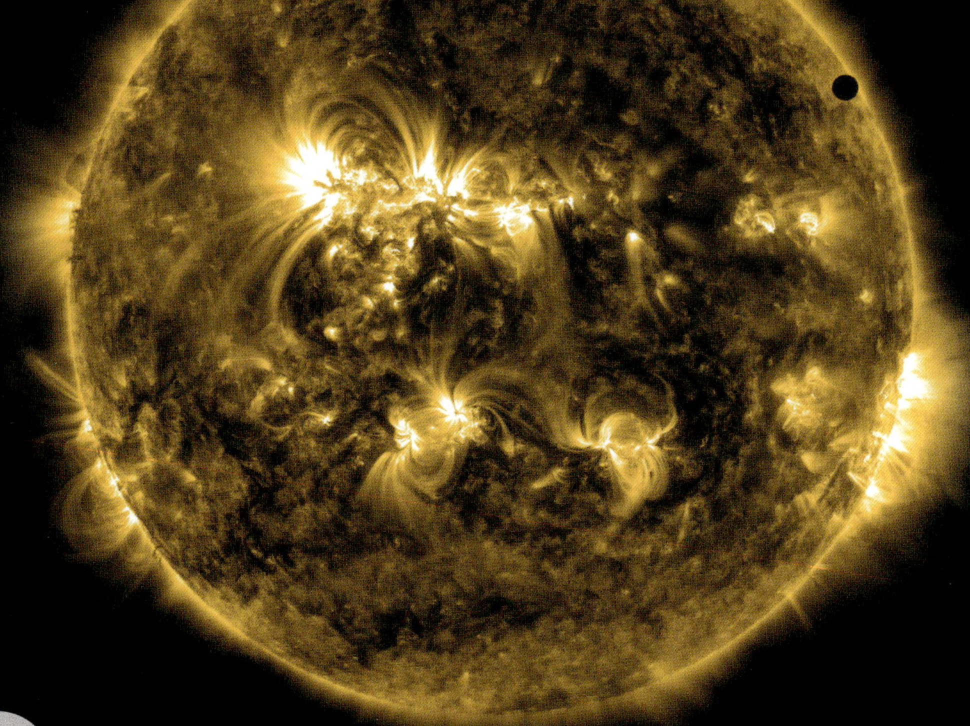

Finding a Solution

There was one possible solution for these problems: what if Earth and the other planets actually orbited the sun? A few ancient philosophers, such as Aristarchus of Samos (c. 310–c. 230 BCE), had proposed this, but they were not taken seriously. In the sixteenth century, the Polish astronomer Nicolaus Copernicus (1473–1543) published a book that took the world by storm. He brought together centuries of observations and calculations to figure out a model that seemed to match what people had observed. However, it took more than a century for his ideas to be widely accepted.

This illustration shows Copernicus' model of the solar system with the sun at the center.

Space Science

Although he was not the first to figure out the order of the planets, Ptolemy was right in saying that Venus and Mercury were closer to Earth than the sun was. Very rarely, Venus passes exactly between Earth and the sun and can be seen as a black dot moving across the face of the sun. This is called a transit, and the Persian philosopher and physician Avicenna (980–1037 CE) may have witnessed this as early as 1032 CE. The transits prove that Venus is closer to Earth than the sun is.

Spotting Phenomena

The telescope was invented at the beginning of the seventeenth century, and for the first time, astronomers could see phenomena such as mountains on the moon, the moons of Jupiter, and Saturn's rings. The telescope also helped reveal more about the sun. For example, astronomers were able to see sunspots more clearly. These had been seen before, but were usually thought to be objects transiting the sun. The scientist Galileo Galilei (1564–1642) studied them and realized that they must be on the surface of the sun.

It must have been astonishing to see Saturn's rings when telescopes were first invented in the seventeenth century.

Calculations and Discoveries

In 1672, Jean-Dominique Cassini (1625–1712) calculated the distance to Mars. Based on this, he came up with an accurate figure for the distance to the sun. Many discoveries during this period had to do with analyzing the sun's light. For example, in about 1666, Sir Isaac Newton (1642–1727) used a prism to show that the sun's light could be split into rays of different colors.

Finding Hidden Light

In 1800, scientist William Herschel (1738–1822) took Newton's theory a step further when he discovered infrared radiation. There are many types of electromagnetic radiation, and the light that we see is just one of them. Types of electromagnetic radiation are classified by their wavelength. Herschel was using colored filters on his telescope when he discovered that some colors made the telescope heat up more than others. He had discovered infrared light, which is invisible to the human eye.

Studying Light

In the nineteenth century, astronomers began to use spectroscopy to study light. All substances absorb light at particular wavelengths, and by studying the light that reflects from an object, scientists can learn what it is made of. Joseph von Fraunhofer (1787–1826) found lines in the spectrum of sunlight that corresponded with elements in its atmosphere.

This enormous telescope was constructed by William Herschel to help him study the night sky.

Space Science

It is incredibly dangerous to stare directly at the sun, and you should never look at the sun through binoculars or a telescope. Its light can permanently damage your eyes. Astronomers such as Galileo were able to study the sun by looking at it at sunrise or sunset, when its light is not as dangerous. Many of them also used their telescopes to project the sun's image onto a white card, which they could look at safely.

YOUR MISSION

Astronomers such as Galileo were able to find out more about the solar system because of the invention of technology such as the telescope. In the future, technology may advance to a point at which we could travel closer to stars like the sun to learn more about them. Imagine you are in charge of designing a manned spacecraft suitable for flying close to stars to observe them. What would be the key requirements of your design? Consider these challenges:

- Stars give off intense light
- Stars emit dangerous heat

Chapter 2

INSIDE THE SUN

The Earth and the other planets are spheres, but they are not just simple lumps of rock or balls of liquid and gas. Each planet has its own internal structure, with a central core and various different layers. The sun is no different. Over the years, astronomers have been able to identify several different layers within the sun.

What Lies Beneath?

No one has even seen below Earth's crust, but scientists are fairly sure that beneath it is a mantle of dense rock that can behave like a fluid, then a liquid metal outer core surrounding a solid iron inner core. Scientists can figure out this structure by studying the way that seismic waves from earthquakes travel through Earth. In the same way, we cannot see inside the sun, so astronomers must use the available clues to figure out what is inside it.

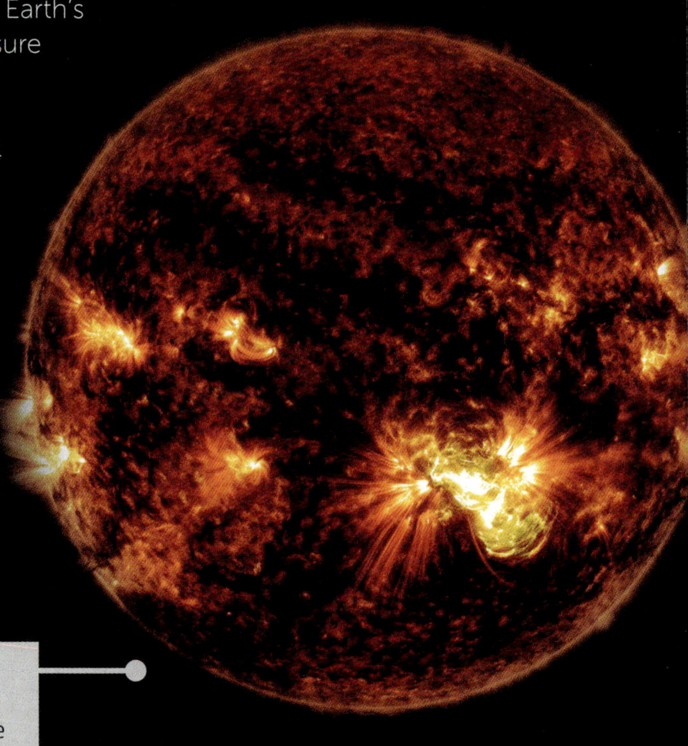

This photograph of the sun shows dramatic solar flares (see opposite) erupting from the surface of the giant ball of gas.

Changes Inside

The sun's surface is a busy place. Sunspots appear and fade away, patterns of granulation constantly change, and flares and eruptions burst from its surface into its atmosphere. These changes are the result of something happening inside the sun that we cannot see. The challenge for scientists is to figure out what could be causing these dramatic and violent changes.

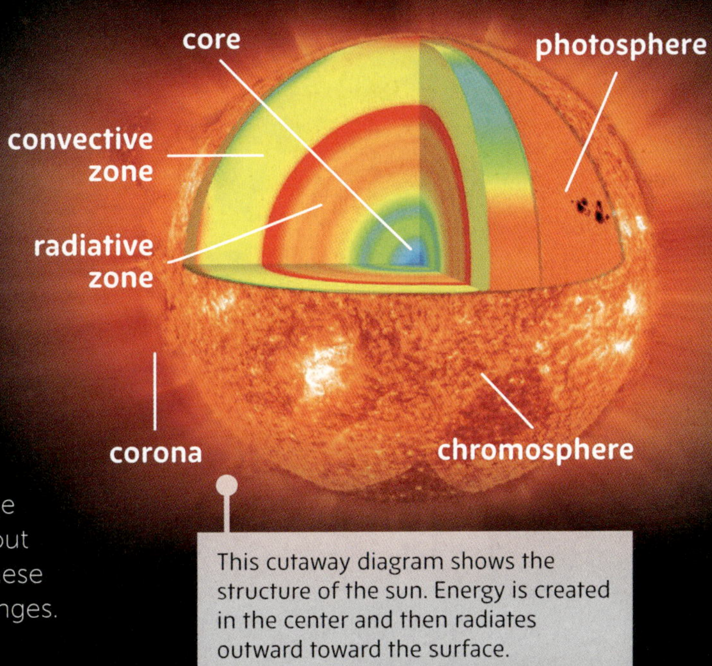

This cutaway diagram shows the structure of the sun. Energy is created in the center and then radiates outward toward the surface.

Figuring Out the Sun

By observing the sun's surface and atmosphere, astronomers have figured out the basic structure of the sun. At the center is the core, where the sun's energy is generated. Outside that is the radiative zone, where energy from the core is carried outward into the convective zone. Then comes the photosphere, where the energy mostly takes the form of visible light. Above that are the chromosphere, corona, and heliosphere.

SPACE SCIENCE

Many scientists create computer models of the sun to test theories about how it works. First, they make sure that their virtual sun obeys the known laws of physics. Then they make a computer model that recreates a process they believe happens inside the sun. The computer shows what the effects on the sun's visible surface would be. If these match up with actual observations of the sun, the theory may be right.

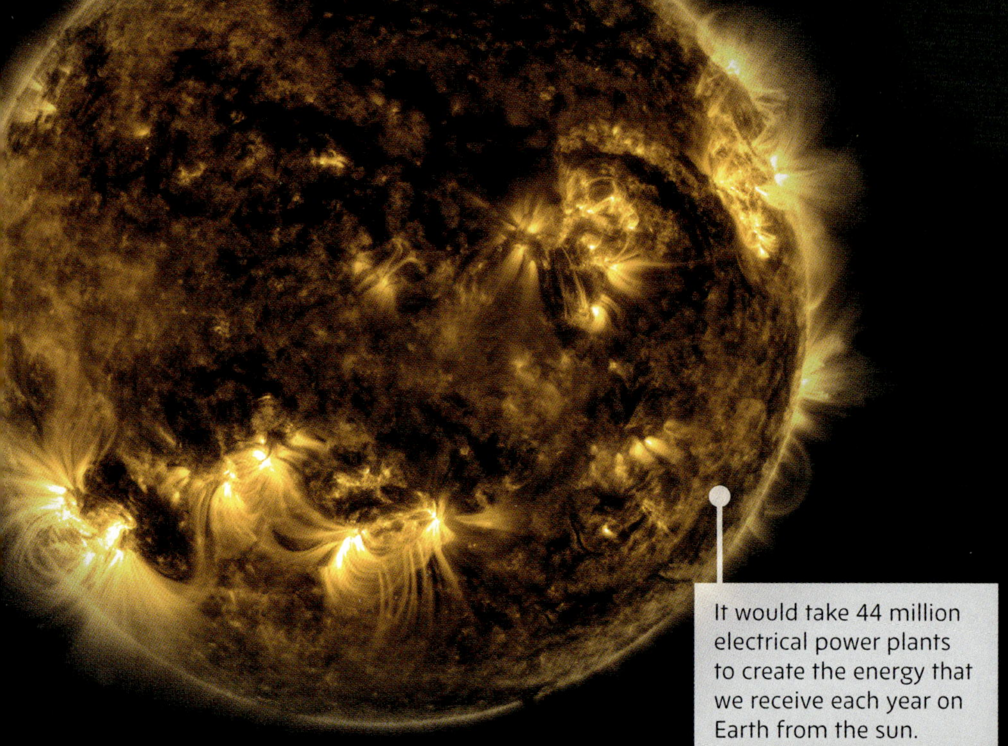

It would take 44 million electrical power plants to create the energy that we receive each year on Earth from the sun.

Not a Solid Sun

Unlike Earth, the sun is not solid. Instead, it is completely made up of gas and a state of matter called plasma. The density and temperature of the gas and plasma change as you move through the inside of the sun, and this is how we separate the different layers. At the center of the sun is the core, which is the densest part. The force of gravity causes all the other layers to press down on the core, which is why it is so dense—it is about 20 times denser than iron. The core is also incredibly hot—around 27,000,000 degrees Fahrenheit (15,000,000 °C)!

Outside the Core

The radiative zone (also called the radiation zone) is located outside the core. There, energy generated by the core is moved toward the outer layers of the sun through a process called radiation. There are three ways to transfer heat or energy from one place to another. In conduction and convection, energy is transferred between particles in a solid, liquid, or gas. Radiation, on the other hand, does not require contact between the heat source and the heated object. This is why we feel the sun's heat, even though we are not touching it.

Studying the Inside

One way that scientists study the interior of the sun is through a technique called helioseismology. The motion of the matter in the sun's outer layers produces sound waves. The waves are usually trapped inside the sun and bounce back and forth between its different parts. Scientists can study the way they bounce to learn about the temperature, density, and movement of energy inside the sun.

On a sunny day, radiation allows us to feel the warmth of the sun's rays on our skin.

SPACE SCIENCE

You probably know that all matter can exist in one of three states: solid, liquid, or gas. However, there is also a fourth state of matter. Plasma is similar to gas, but the atoms are different. Most atoms have a nucleus with electrons whizzing around it. In a plasma, the electrons are not bound to the nucleus, so they can move freely around the system. Gases can become plasmas when enough energy is added for the transformation to occur.

Cooling Down

Once energy travels out of the radiative zone, it moves into a cooler area called the convective zone. Where the core meets the radiative zone, the temperature decreases to about 12,500,000 degrees Fahrenheit (6,944,000 °C). By the time energy reaches the convective zone, it cools to about 3,600,000 degrees Fahrenheit (2,000,000 °C). As a result of this lower temperature, energy cannot travel as efficiently by radiation. Instead, it moves outward in a process known as convection.

Hot and Cold Movements

Convection is what happens when a pan of water is put on the stove to boil. When the particles in the liquid are heated, they move faster and take up more space. This makes the hot areas of the liquid less dense than the cold areas. The hot liquid rises and the denser cold liquid moves to take its place. Eventually, this movement of hot and cold liquids heats everything in the pan. The same thing happens to the plasma in the convective zone of the sun.

What We Can See

Although the sun is not solid, in the inner layers the gas is so dense that we cannot see through it. Above the convection zone, however, is the photosphere, which is the first layer that we can study with telescopes and other tools. When looking at the photosphere we can see a pattern called granulation. Although it is relatively cool in the photosphere—about 10,000 degrees Fahrenheit (5,538 °C), the gas is thin enough for radiation to take place again. Most of the heat and light that we receive on Earth was released by the photosphere.

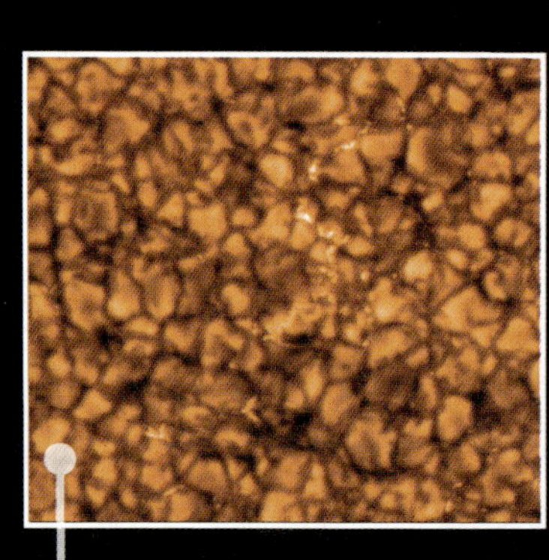

This granulation pattern appears on the surface of the sun.

SPACE SCIENCE

In the radiative zone, energy from the sun's core is transferred from place to place by radiation. However, radiation does not just move in a single direction. The energy is passed randomly, sometimes moving outward, and other times moving inward or side-to-side. It can take more than 170,000 years for energy to get out of the radiation zone! It moves much more quickly through the convection zone, and can get to the top of the zone in a little more than a week.

Making a Long Journey

The energy that reaches us on Earth has had a very long journey through the sun's layers, followed by a much shorter one (about eight minutes) through space at the speed of light. Where did it come from in the first place? The answer lies in a process called nuclear fusion, where atoms are ripped apart and put back together to form new substances.

Heat and Pressure

In the sun's core, the temperature and pressure are high enough to destroy the internal structure of atoms. Most atoms are made up of a nucleus containing protons and neutrons, with electrons surrounding them. The sun is mainly made up of hydrogen atoms, which have one proton and one electron. When they interact with each other under extreme pressure, two nuclei can fuse, creating atoms of helium, which each have two protons in the nucleus. It takes several intermediate steps, but the helium atoms at the end have less mass than the two hydrogen atoms that started the process. The difference in mass is converted to energy, which then starts its journey out of the sun.

How Is Energy Made?

For a long time, scientists did not know how the sun created energy. New Zealand-born Ernest Rutherford (1871–1937) thought it might be caused by radioactive decay. It was a British physicist, Arthur Eddington (1882–1944), who first suggested in the 1920s that the temperature and pressure inside the sun could produce nuclear fusion. He drew on Albert Einstein's work to help him formulate his ideas. Scientists' observations of the sun since the 1920s have supported Eddington's theory.

Albert Einstein (1879–1955) created an important theory about the relation between mass and energy.

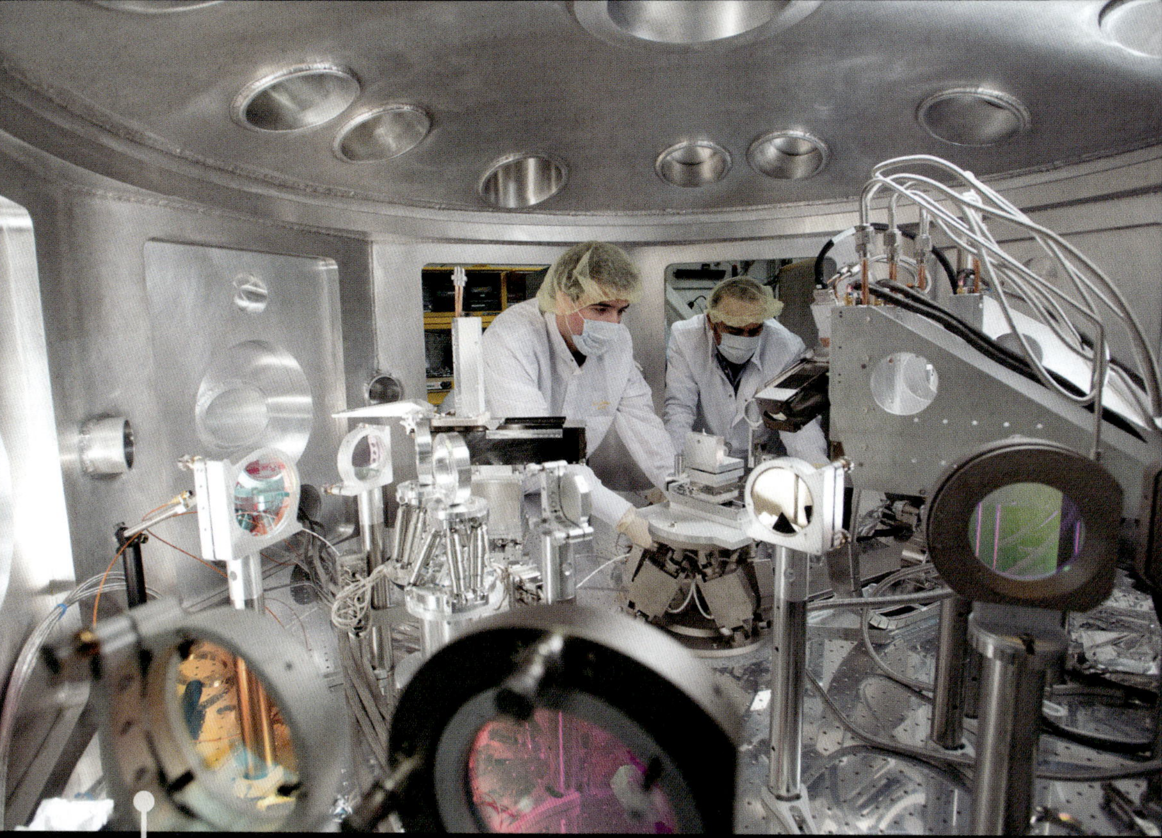

Scientists are investigating the extremely hot matter at the centers of stars to try to recreate the nuclear fusion process that powers the sun.

SPACE SCIENCE

Scientists have been trying to create nuclear fusion in laboratories, because it is a potential source of clean energy that could eventually replace fossil fuels, such as oil and natural gas. However, we cannot recreate all the conditions that allow fusion in the sun's core. We can heat the plasma to incredibly high temperatures, but must use strong magnetic fields to contain it. So far, the energy required to produce fusion on Earth has nearly always been higher than the energy it generates.

Spotting Dark Spots

From time to time, dark spots appear on the sun's visible surface: the photosphere. These are called sunspots, and they have been observed for many years. For example, Chinese astronomers recorded sunspots more than 2,000 years ago. However, it took a long time for these spots to be understood. Most people who saw sunspots assumed they were objects passing in front of the sun. The Catholic Church's teachings at the time stated that the sun was perfect and unchanging —it would have seemed impossible that it could have had blemishes on its surface.

Dark spots on the surface of the sun are clearly visible in this photograph of it.

On the Surface

Eventually, most scientists accepted Galileo's theory that sunspots were actually on the surface of the sun, but they still did not know what caused them. In 1848, the US scientist Joseph Henry (1797–1878) showed that sunspots were cooler than the surrounding areas. It was not until the twentieth century that astronomers realized that sunspots were caused by magnetic activity.

Bending and Twisting Magnetism

Deep inside the sun, magnetic fields are constantly being generated. As they rise through the sun's layers, they can bend or twist. Measurements of the sun's magnetism have shown that sunspots are areas of concentrated magnetic fields. Scientists used a tool called a spectroheliograph to detect magnetic fields on the sun.

Here Today, Gone Tomorrow

One thing about sunspots that has been known for centuries is that they come and go. A sunspot can appear for as little as an hour or two, though some last for several months. Sometimes very few sunspots can be seen; at other times there are many more. Over the centuries astronomers have made detailed records of sunspots, and we now know that the number of sunspots rises and falls over an 11-year cycle.

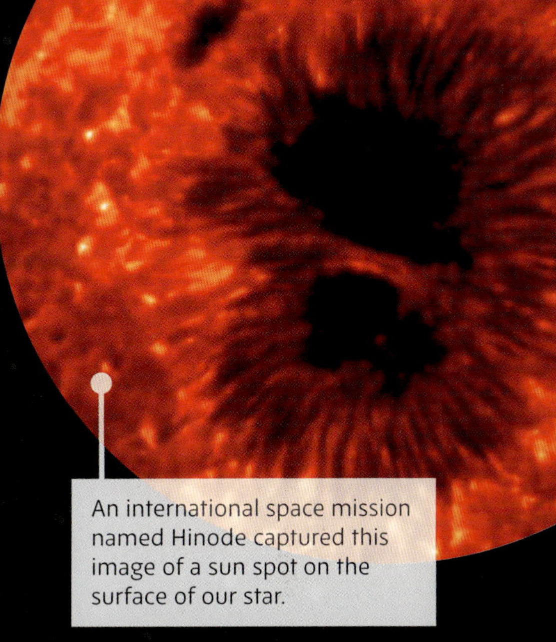

An international space mission named Hinode captured this image of a sun spot on the surface of our star.

Space Science

The average temperature of the photosphere is about 10,000 degrees Fahrenheit (5,538 °C) but sunspots are only about 6,000 degrees Fahrenheit (3,316 °C). For the sun, that is quite cool but it is still hot enough to boil iron! The darkest part of a sunspot, at the center, is called the umbra (the Latin word for shadow). The lighter region that surrounds it is called the penumbra.

Your Mission

Being able to create nuclear fusion to provide us with sustainable energy would be an enormous achievement and could solve our energy issues. However, it is extremely difficult and is still in the experimental stage. Imagine it is your mission to persuade investors to commit to a program of labs devoted to the creation of nuclear fusion. The investors could put forward the below arguments against the project. In response, what would your counterarguments be?

- Fossil fuels already exist, humanmade nuclear fusion does not
- The cost would be too expensive and it would take too long
- There is no guarantee of success
- We should invest only in other existing sources of sustainable energy, such as wind power

Chapter 3

THE SUN'S ATMOSPHERE

Just like Earth, the sun also has its own atmosphere. Although there is no solid boundary, the layers above the photosphere are usually known as the "solar atmosphere." They include the chromosphere and the corona. They are one of the easier regions of the sun to study because they can be viewed with many different types of telescopes.

A Thick Layer of Gas

The chromosphere is a layer of gas that is about 1,250 miles (2,000 km) thick. It is much less dense than the photosphere, and without special equipment, it cannot normally be seen because the brightness of the photosphere drowns it out. In the chromosphere, energy is emitted as red light. Scientists can get a good look at the chromosphere by filtering out all other wavelengths of light, which leaves only the red light from the chromosphere.

The sun's corona is its thinnest layer. It is so thin and faint that it can be seen only during a solar eclipse, shown above, or by using a special telescope.

Other Layers

Within the sun's chromosphere, the temperature can rise to about 36,000 degrees Fahrenheit (20,000 °C). A thin transition zone lies between the chromosphere and the corona, where the temperature rises even more, to about 1,800,000 degrees Fahrenheit (1,000,000 °C). The heliosphere is the outer atmosphere of the sun and extends beyond the planets, but the corona is considered the outermost layer.

Studying with Rays

Scientists can use radio waves, gamma rays, and x-rays to study the sun's outer layers. Even so, there are still mysteries. For example, they are still not sure why the temperature is so high in these regions that are incredibly far way from the heat-producing core. Astronomers are researching theories that might link the sun's magnetic field to the temperature rise.

These jets on the sun are known as spicules. They combine with energy from the sun's magnetic field and shoot outward from the star's surface.

Space Science

The chromosphere appears to have a jagged, constantly changing outer layer. This is caused by long, thin "fingers" of glowing gas that rise from the bottom. They are called spicules. It takes them about 10 to 15 minutes to rise to the top of the chromosphere, traveling at a speed of 12 miles per second (19 kps), and then sink back down again. Gas from the chromosphere also forms prominences, which are large loops that rise more than 100,000 miles (160,934 km) above the sun's surface.

A Hot Solar Wind

The sun's hot corona is the source of a phenomenon known as the solar wind. This is a stream of charged particles that flows out in all directions, extending far beyond Neptune. The area where the solar wind blows is called the heliosphere, and it is like a huge bubble, held within the ambient gas, dust, and magnetic fields of the galaxy.

Full of Energy

The particles of the solar wind can escape the sun's gravity because the high temperature of the corona gives them a lot of energy. They travel extremely fast: anywhere between 670,000 and 1.8 million miles per hour (1,080,000 and 2,900,000 kph). The speed of the solar wind changes a lot, and in places high-speed wind can catch up with low-speed wind.

Coronal holes are areas of open magnetic field on the sun's surface from which solar wind particles stream into space.

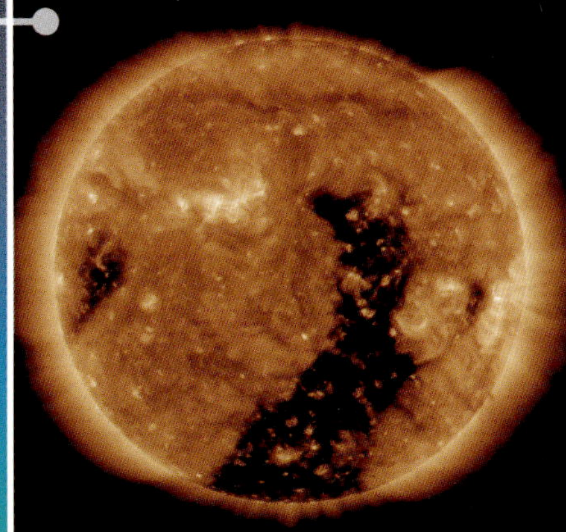

Lights and Storms

Earth has an invisible magnetic field surrounding it, which protects us from some types of solar radiation. When the solar wind hits Earth's magnetic field, most of it is deflected and travels around the planet instead of reaching the surface. However, the solar wind still has an effect. Often, when it interacts with the magnetic field, it causes the auroras, better known as the Northern and Southern Lights. It also causes geomagnetic storms occasionally, which can disrupt satellites and electronic devices.

Protected by the Field

We are lucky to have our magnetic field to protect us. Planets with no magnetic fields (or very weak ones) can have their atmosphere stripped away by the force of the solar wind. For example, Mars's weak magnetic field is not strong enough to provide much protection, and the solar wind has stripped away much of the atmosphere that it once had.

This beautiful photograph of the Northern Lights was taken in Iceland, in northern Europe.

Space Science

In 1997, the National Aeronautics and Space Administration (NASA) launched the Advanced Composition Explorer (ACE) spacecraft to study several topics, including the solar wind. It orbits in a position where the force of Earth's gravity and the sun's are about equal, approximately 1 million miles (1,600,000 km) from Earth. It has a variety of tools for monitoring the solar wind, and it provides data that helps scientists forecast solar storms.

Flaring Up

Seen from Earth, the sun appears constant and unchanging, but the sun's surface and atmosphere are regions of sometimes violent activity. One example of this is a solar flare: an enormous explosion that takes place on the surface of the sun. During a solar flare, sections of the sun's matter are heated to millions of degrees in just a few minutes, releasing huge amounts of energy. The energy can take the form of gamma rays, x-rays, and charged particles.

When a burst of solar material leaps off the surface of the sun it is known as a prominence eruption.

Huge Explosions

For many years astronomers thought that solar flares were the main type of explosion on the sun. In the 1970s however, scientists found evidence of the existence of a much bigger type of explosion: the coronal mass ejection (CME). A CME occurs when a solar prominence erupts and sends a large amount of matter out into the solar system. When a CME collides with Earth's magnetosphere, it can shut down electricity grids, as well as interfere with radio communications and damage satellites.

Difficult to See

It took so long to discover CMEs because the corona is difficult to observe from Earth. Normally, it is visible only during a total solar eclipse, and these events are rare. Astronomers can study the corona at other times by using a coronagraph, which creates an artificial eclipse by blocking out the bright disc of the sun. However, coronagraphs on ground-based telescopes show only the innermost part of the corona; the rest is drowned out by the brightness of the sky. From space you can see more of the corona, so spacecraft are crucial for studying this volatile region.

This photograph shows a CME blasting billions of tons of solar matter out into space.

Space Science

Both solar flares and CMEs are related to the same magnetic activity that causes sunspots. For example, solar flares usually occur near sunspots. Solar flares and CMEs also follow the 11-year solar cycle. At the solar minimum, when there are few sunspots, there is about one CME per week. At the solar maximum, when sunspots are at their peak, there are two or three CMEs per day.

Your Mission

You have been charged with planning a program of CME observation from space. As part of your planning, you must consider the following:

- When the program would need to be most active, and the observation more intense
- The equipment needed to run the program
- The STEM skills you would look for in team members who would help run the program

Chapter 4

BEGINNINGS AND ENDS

Supernovae is the name we give to the explosive deaths of massive stars, like this one named N132D.

Stars are not living things, but the terms used to describe them often make it sound as though they are. We use terms such as "birth," "life," and "death," but these are not meant literally—they are just a way of making difficult concepts more understandable. Stars are even described as having a "life cycle" or an "evolution," which means that over the course of many years, they are formed, they change, and eventually, they die.

One of Many

The sun is just one of billions of trillions of stars in the universe, and it is following the same series of stages as all other stars. It began in a giant cloud of gas and dust called a nebula. A nebula can have enough raw material to make thousands of stars. Inside the nebula, the gas and dust starts to clump together. Eventually these growing clumps form protostars, which start to heat up.

Critical Mass

What happens next depends on how big the protostar is. It must have a certain amount of mass in order to create temperatures high enough for nuclear fusion to start. If the protostar has enough mass —approximately 8 percent of the mass of our sun or more—then the core will heat up to millions of degrees Fahrenheit. The process of nuclear fusion will start, and the star will begin to shine. Once this happens, the star is called a "main sequence star," and it will remain this way until its fuel begins to run out. About 90 percent of the stars in the universe, including our sun, are main sequence stars.

SPACE SCIENCE

If a protostar is not massive enough for nuclear fusion, it will never begin to shine. It will become what is known as a brown dwarf, and over the next few billion years, it will slowly cool down. The smallest brown dwarfs are only about twice the mass of Jupiter. These "failed stars" were just a theory until they were actually discovered in 1995. Now some astronomers think that there might be as many brown dwarfs in the universe as there are stars.

This artist's image shows a brown dwarf, a "failed star" that is not big enough to begin nuclear fusion in its core. This is the characteristic that defines a star.

Not Forever

Stars do not live forever. The nuclear fusion taking place in their cores presses outward, balancing the force of gravity pulling inward. This makes the star stable, but eventually the fuel will run out, and the star will "die." How long this takes depends on how big the star is. A really massive star has a lot of fuel, but it also has stronger gravity, which makes the core hotter. This means that the star will burn through its fuel a lot faster than a smaller star would.

How Long Will It Live?

Our sun, which is a medium-sized star, will exist as a main sequence star for about 10 billion years. However, a star about 10 times as massive as the sun will last for only about 20 million years. At the other end of the spectrum, a star with half the mass of the sun, known as a red dwarf, can probably last for 80 to 100 billion years, which is much longer than the universe has existed.

This artist's impression shows a red dwarf. They often have huge prominences and a lot of dark sunspots, as shown here.

Giant to Dwarf

The sun formed about 4.6 billion years ago so it is nearly halfway through its life. In billions of years, when its fuel starts to run out, the core will begin to contract and get hotter. The outer layers of the sun will expand, becoming so big that they extend past the current orbit of Mars. Earth would be swallowed up, and destroyed. At that point the sun would be known as a red giant. Eventually the outer layers will drift away, leaving the dying core to cool and dim, becoming a white dwarf. When the core stops shining altogether it is called a black dwarf. However, white dwarfs cool so slowly that the universe is not yet old enough for any black dwarfs to exist.

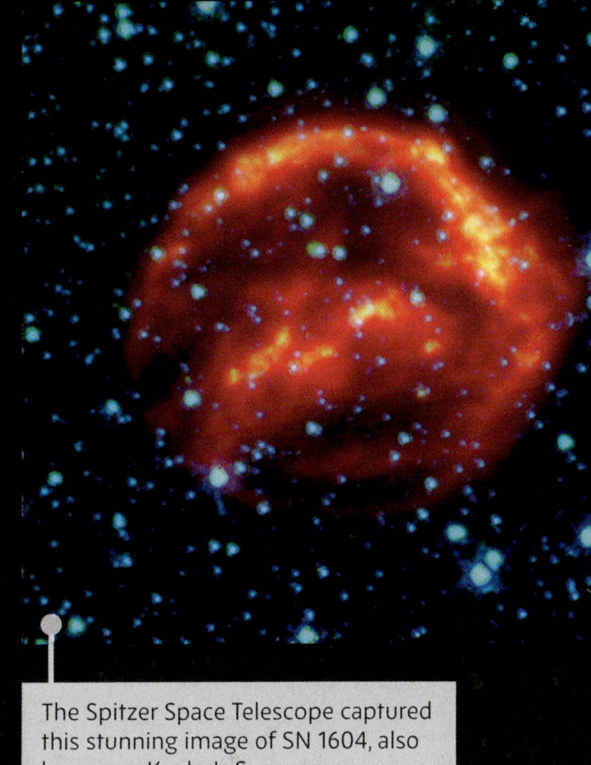

The Spitzer Space Telescope captured this stunning image of SN 1604, also known as Kepler's Supernova.

SPACE SCIENCE

If the sun were a lot larger than it is, it would not eventually turn into a red giant. Instead, it would burn through its fuel much more quickly and end up with a helium core, which would fuse into heavier and heavier elements, surrounded by a huge shell of cooling, expanding gas. Eventually the element iron would form in the core and further nuclear fusion would cease. At this point, the gravity of the core would cause it to collapse under its own weight and blow itself apart in a massive explosion—a supernova.

The Solar Cycle

In addition to its life cycle, the sun goes through another, much shorter cycle called the solar cycle. Approximately every 11 years, the sun reaches a peak of magnetic activity. This peak is called the solar maximum and during this time there are visible sunspots nearly all the time. At the opposite end of the cycle, the solar minimum, sunspots are rare and only last a short time.

Following the Cycle

Other types of solar activity, such as solar flares and CMEs, are also caused by the sun's magnetism. They also follow the solar cycle and are much more common around the solar maximum. However, you have probably never noticed the changes in the sun's output. Over the course of a solar cycle, the maximum change in the sun's radiation is less than 0.1 percent of its total output.

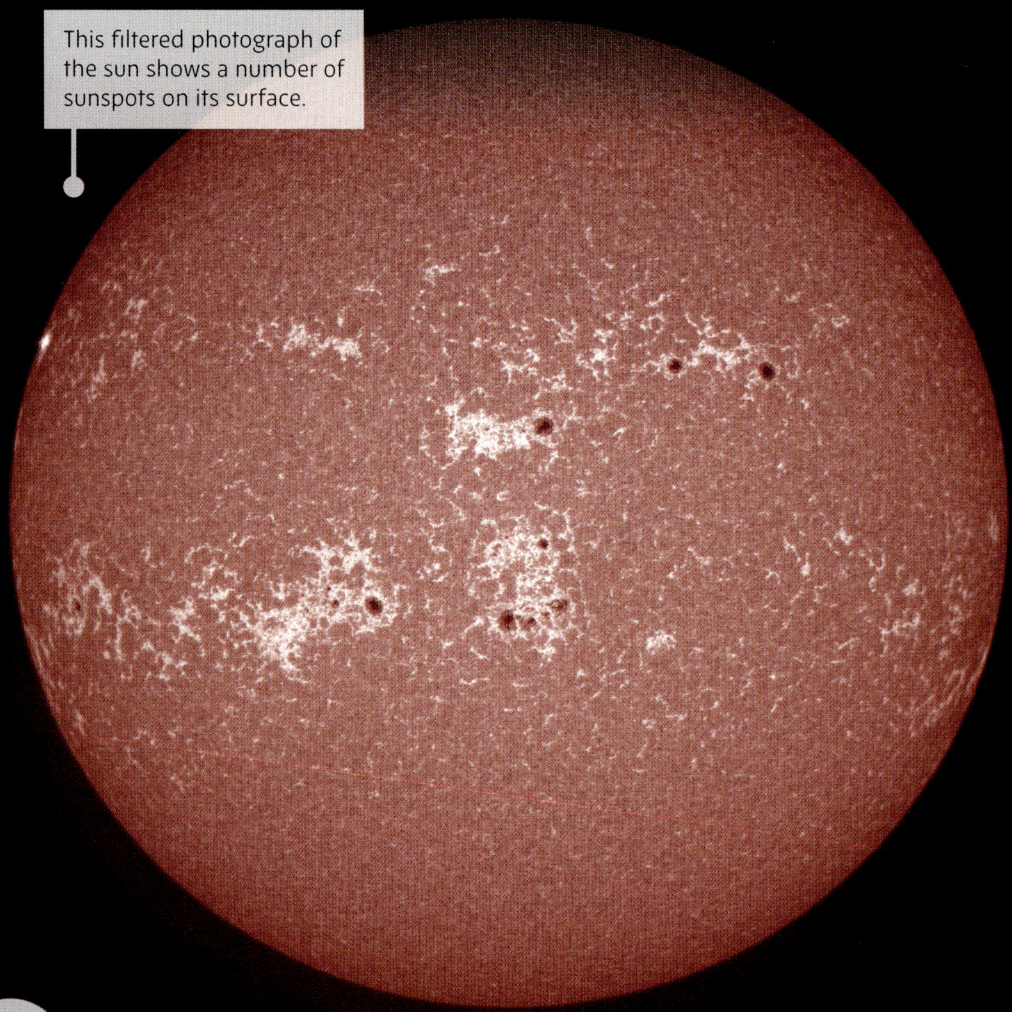

This filtered photograph of the sun shows a number of sunspots on its surface.

Affecting Earth

Even though humans do not notice the sun being any hotter or brighter during the solar maximum, there are still effects felt on Earth. For example, during these periods there are more solar flares and CMEs. These can send radiation toward Earth that damages satellites and spacecraft and can disrupt electronic communications.

Leading to Ice Ages

However, the detailed records of sunspots we have, which go back centuries, show that the sun's output can affect Earth's climate over long periods. Between 1645 and 1714 there were almost no sunspots, and this coincided with the peak of the "Little Ice Age," an unusually cool period that particularly affected Europe and North America from the 1300s to the 1800s.

The sun greatly influences our climate and its activity can lead to times of intense cold, which are called ice ages.

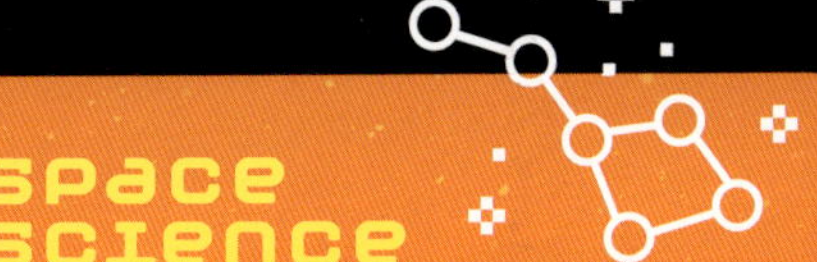

Space Science

One interesting phenomenon is that tree rings seem to show evidence of sunspot activity. If you slice through a tree's trunk, you will see a growth ring corresponding to each year of its life. During a year when conditions are good, a tree will grow more, resulting in a thick ring. In a bad year, for example, during a drought, the ring will be thinner. Some evidence shows that tree rings seem to follow an 11-year cycle, corresponding to the solar cycle, but scientists are not yet sure exactly why this is.

Your Mission

You are heading up a mission into outer space to seek out stars of different ages. You will monitor their structure and behavior. During the mission, which of the below would you be most interested to discover and why?:

- Stars at their point of "birth"
- Main-sequence stars
- Dying stars

Chapter 5 STUDYING ECLIPSES

While Earth travels around the sun, the moon is traveling around Earth. Once a month, the moon passes between Earth and the sun. If they are aligned just right, the moon will block the sun's light, causing a shadow to fall on part of Earth. This is called an eclipse. During a total solar eclipse, the sky slowly dims until it becomes dark, and the temperature drops. For people thousands of years ago, who did not understand how it happened, eclipses could be terrifying.

This image captures a partial eclipse of the sun, with only part of the star covered.

Different Types of Eclipses

Not all eclipses completely block out the sun, though. There are four types of solar eclipses: total, partial, annular, and hybrid. In a total eclipse, everything lines up perfectly and the moon completely blocks out the sun. In a partial eclipse, the moon and the sun do not quite line up, so the moon only partially covers the disc of the sun, leaving a crescent shape.

Once a Year

Sometimes the moon is slightly farther away from Earth than at other times, making it appear smaller in the sky. This can lead to an annular eclipse, when a bright ring of sun is visible around the moon. A hybrid eclipse appears as a total eclipse from some parts of Earth's surface and as an annular eclipse from other regions before becoming a total eclipse.

Just a Few

The moon does not orbit exactly in line with Earth's orbit around the sun. If it did, we would have a solar eclipse every month. The moon's orbit is slightly tilted, so we get eclipses only when the two paths intersect. In most years there are only a few solar eclipses, and each one is only visible from a relatively small area of Earth's surface.

Writings and drawings from the Middle Ages record solar eclipses, which must have seemed both terrifying and fascinating.

SPACE SCIENCE

Earth is a great place for viewing solar eclipses. Someone living on Mercury or Venus would never see an eclipse because these planets have no moons to block the sun. Mars's moons are too small to cause a total eclipse. The sun is about 400 times bigger in diameter than our moon, but it is also about 400 times farther away. This means that the sun and moon appear almost exactly the same size in the sky, causing amazing total eclipses.

Rare Eclipses

Total solar eclipses are one of the most amazing phenomena seen on Earth, but they are rare. They happen about once every 18 months, but can be seen only from specific locations. During a total eclipse, the moon's shadow follows a path about 10,000 miles (16,000 km) long but only 100 miles (161 km) wide. Only people within that area will see the sun become completely covered.

Stages of a Total Eclipse

During a total solar eclipse, the first thing visible from Earth will be a tiny bite out of the side of the sun. This is called "first contact." Over the next hour and a half or so, the moon covers more and more of the sun, until only a small crescent is left. The light on Earth is dimmer at that point. A few minutes before totality, the crescent is reduced to a few tiny specks of light around the edge, called Baily's Beads. When only one bright "bead" is left, the sun looks like a diamond ring. When the beads disappear and the sun is completely eclipsed, this is "second contact."

This image shows the diamond ring effect that takes place at the beginning and end of totality during a total solar eclipse (see opposite).

The Final Stages

During totality, the sun's corona shines around the disc of the moon. Totality lasts for only a few minutes, and then the eclipse reaches "third contact" when the photosphere starts to emerge from behind the sun. The diamond ring effect may be visible again before the moon moves farther away. "Fourth contact" occurs when the full disc of the sun is seen again.

During a total solar eclipse, the sun's corona appears as a crown of white flares. The red spots around the edge are Baily's Beads.

SPACE SCIENCE

It is never safe to look directly at the sun, except for during the few moments of totality. Even when 99 percent of the sun's surface is obscured, the remaining part is still bright enough to damage your eyes. Sunglasses are not enough to protect your eyes; you need a specially-made filter to watch a solar eclipse. The safest way of viewing an eclipse is by making a pinhole in a piece of cardboard, and letting the sun shine through that hole onto a white piece of paper, where you will see a projected image of the sun.

This artist's image shows the Solar Dynamics Observatory (SDO) spacecraft as it faces the sun during its observations of it.

Studying the Sun's Corona

A total solar eclipse offers a rare chance to study the sun's corona. In fact, it is the only time that the corona is visible from Earth with the naked eye. Amateur observers can also see other things during a total eclipse. For example, in the first few seconds of totality, a red streak is often visible along the side of the moon. This is the reddish light of the chromosphere, which normally cannot be seen because of the brightness of the photosphere.

Earth and Space

Although the corona is not visible from Earth at other times, spacecraft such as the SDO or the Solar and Heliospheric Observatory (SOHO) can see it at all times. However, the coronagraphs that they use block out the innermost section of the corona, so scientists make use of solar eclipses to get a good view of this part. Another good reason for studying the corona from Earth during eclipses is that it is much cheaper and more flexible to send a team of scientists to view an eclipse than it is to launch a spacecraft!

Measuring and Monitoring

During a solar eclipse, astronomers can measure the temperature of the corona by using spectroscopy. They can also look for vibrations in the corona that might give a clue as to the reason for its incredibly high temperatures. Advances in technology mean that computer images are now able to bring out low-contrast features that had not been seen in previous eclipses.

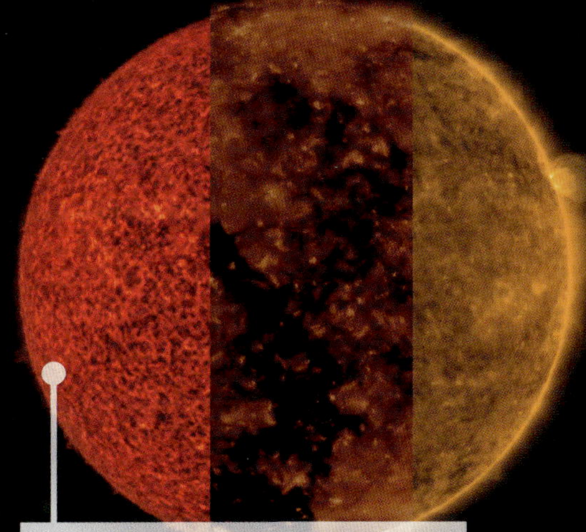

Modern high-tech studies of the sun now allow us to compare its different phases and features.

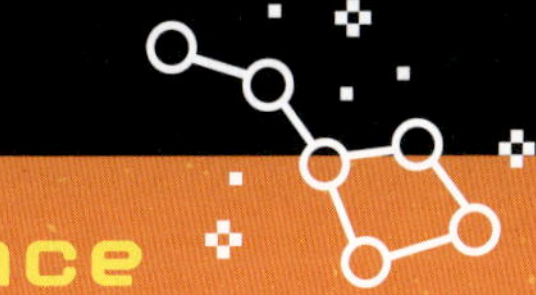

Space Science

In the days before spacecraft, eclipses were the only way to study the corona, and it was during an eclipse that helium was discovered. In 1868, while observing an eclipse in India, French astronomer Pierre Janssen (1824–1907) used a spectrograph and found a bright yellow line in a solar prominence. It was caused by an undiscovered element, which was called helium. Helium was not found on Earth until 1895. In 1930, an eclipse gave a German astronomer the evidence he needed to estimate the temperature of the corona.

YOUR MISSION

You are on a mission to discover what solar eclipses are like in other solar systems. To effectively carry out your mission, consider the below:

» Where you would position yourself to study an eclipse
» Equipment you would use to record an eclipse

Chapter 6

ALWAYS MORE MISSIONS

At any given time there are several different spacecraft studying the sun. Each has its own goals, along with tools specially designed to get the data they need. Here are just a few of them.

ACE: This NASA probe studies particles coming both from the sun and from interstellar sources. It measures and compares the composition of the corona, solar wind, and other types of matter.

Hinode: This probe was launched by the Japanese Aerospace Exploration Agency (JAXA) with collaboration from NASA and the United Kingdom (UK). It has an optical telescope that observes solar magnetic fields, as well as an x-ray telescope and an ultraviolet (UV) imaging spectrometer for studying the corona. It was designed to learn more about the heating of the corona, as well as the causes of mysterious solar flares and the sun's magnetic fields.

SOHO: This incredibly successful joint project between NASA and the European Space Agency (ESA) studies the sun from its core to the outer corona. Its main goals are to use helioseismology to explore the structure of the sun, investigate coronal heating, and find out how the solar wind is produced.

Hinode orbits Earth as it investigates aspects of the sun's activity, such as solar flares.

flow of energy and matter from the sun to Earth.

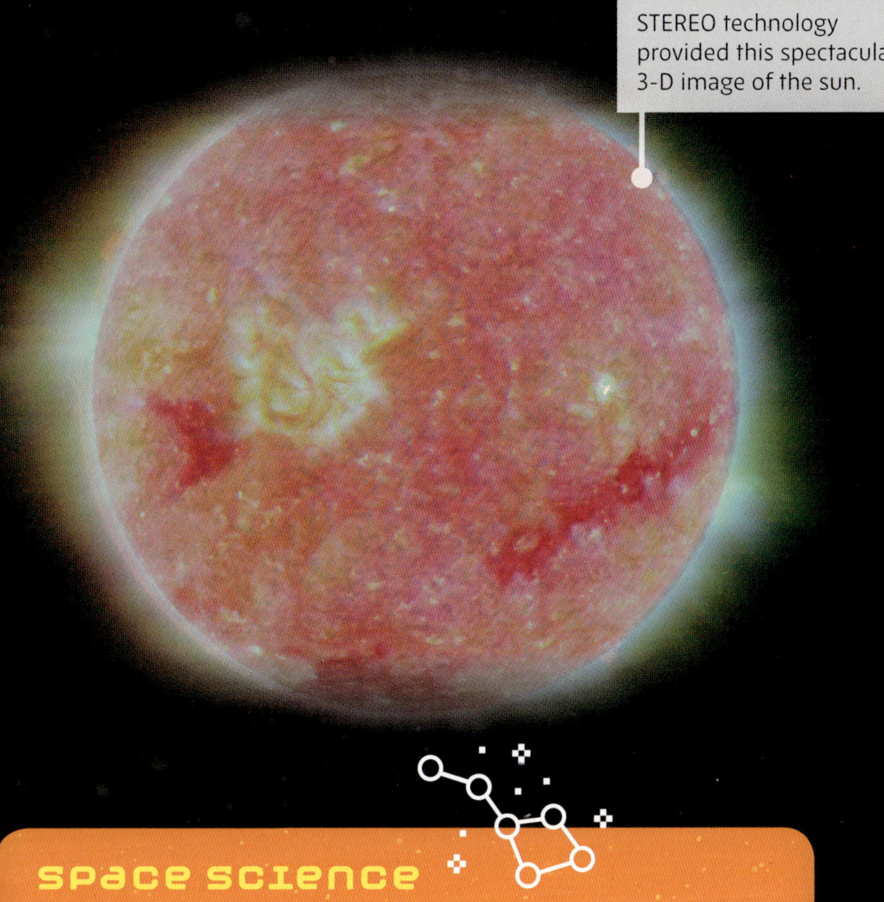

STEREO technology provided this spectacular 3-D image of the sun.

SPACE SCIENCE

Life on Earth has evolved to take advantage of the conditions on our home planet. For example, all life we know of requires water, and there is plenty of water on Earth. Plants and animals are adapted to the fairly narrow range of temperatures found on Earth. However in alien worlds, with other conditions, life might look very different.

These SDO images show a solar flare, which appears as giant flashes of light in the image. Solar flares can disturb technology on Earth.

The Sun and Earth

The sun has a huge effect on life on Earth, and understanding how this works is extremely important. Multiple space probes, among them Cluster-II, Geotail, THEMIS, and TIMED, have been launched to study Earth's atmosphere and magnetosphere in detail. Such probes help scientists learn more about how the sun influences conditions here on Earth.

Studying Space Weather

The energy given off by the sun is variable, meaning that it produces different amounts and types of energy at different times. When experienced on Earth, this variability is known as "space weather." SDO, launched by NASA in 2010, was designed to study the sun from the inside out in order to learn more about the processes inside the sun that create this space weather. Once scientists have a better understanding of how space weather is created, they will be better able to predict it.

Telescopes for the Sun

SDO has an imaging tool that uses helioseismology to "see" beneath the sun's surface. The processes that create the sun's magnetic field begin deep within its interior, and scientists are using the tool to help them understand how the fields are created. The imager is also able to map magnetic fields. SDO also has four different telescopes for observing the sun's surface and atmosphere. The telescopes have different filters, which allow them to view the sun in 10 different wavelengths of light.

Measuring Fluctuations

Another SDO tool is the Extreme Ultraviolet Variability Experiment (EVE). This measures fluctuations in the sun's UV output, which heats Earth's upper atmosphere.

Fluctuations in the sun's activity can have an effect on satellites, including GPS satellites, so predicting them is critical.

SPACE SCIENCE

SDO is part of NASA's "Living With a Star (LWS)" program, which focuses on studying the aspects of the sun that most directly affect life on Earth. For example, the goal of SDO is to learn how solar activity is created, and how this activity creates space weather. Other space probes in this program include the Van Allen Probes, which study the radiation belts that surround Earth.

YOUR MISSION

We know that the sun is one of the key factors that makes life on Earth possible. If you were on a mission to find life on other planets in outer space, what type of star would you expect those planets to be near and why? Give reasons for your answer.

FUTURE MISSIONS

Although scientists have made many incredible discoveries about the sun, there is still a lot to learn and many mysteries to be solved. One of the biggest mysteries is why the corona is so hot, and scientists are also trying to discover the precise causes of solar flares and CMEs. Once they figure this out, they may be able to predict when and where they will take place, and how big they will be. A third big area of study is the cause of the solar cycle.

Answering Questions

Astronomers hope that some of these questions will be answered by the Solar Orbiter, a joint project between NASA and ESA. It is designed to explore how the sun's heliosphere is created and controlled. To do this, it travels closer to the sun than most other spacecraft do. Another NASA probe, Parker Solar Probe has approached even closer as it studies the outer corona. At its closest approach, it will travel only 3.67 million miles (5,900,000 km) from the sun's photosphere. In order to survive the harsh conditions found there, the spacecraft has a solar shadow shield made of a reinforced carbon composite material.

This artist's image shows the Parker Solar Probe, launched in 2018, as it approaches the sun.

New Achievements

The Indian Space Research Organisation (ISRO) celebrated a first for the country when its Mars probe entered orbit around the planet in 2014. Building on that success, its Aditya probe is designed to study the sun's corona, with a focus on CMEs. Aditya was launched in September 2023.

YOUR FUTURE MISSION

Perhaps this book has inspired you to find out more about our sun and other stars in space. Maybe, one day, you'll even carve out a career in space science and make it your mission to explore the mysteries of the universe and unlock its secrets.

GLOSSARY

atmosphere the layer of gases surrounding a planet or moon

atoms the smallest possible units of a chemical element. Atoms are the basis of all matter in the universe

chromosphere the layer of gas that surrounds the sun above the photosphere and below the corona

conduction a way of transferring heat between substances that are in direct contact with each other

convection a way of transferring heat in a liquid or gas; when warmer, less-dense material moves upward and is replaced by cooler, denser material

ecliptic the apparent path of the sun, as seen from Earth against the background of stars

electromagnetic radiation a type of radiation including visible light, radio waves, gamma waves, and x-rays

electrons tiny particles with a negative charge that move outside the nucleus of an atom

equinoxes two times each year when day and night are both 12 hours long

helioseismology the technique of measuring sound waves as they travel through the sun in order to learn about its internal structure

heliosphere the area of space in which the solar wind is felt

infrared radiation a type of electromagnetic energy with a long wavelength, which cannot be seen as visible light

magnetic fields the spaces around magnets in which magnetic forces are active

magnetosphere the region surrounding a planet or other object in which its magnetic field is the dominant magnetic field

mass a measure of how much matter is in an object

nuclear fusion a chemical process in which the nuclei of two or more atoms fuse into a more massive nucleus. This process releases a huge amount of energy

nucleus the center of something, such as an atom

orbit the curved path that one body in space takes around another

photosphere the bright visible surface of the sun

plasma a state of matter in which electrons float free of their nucleus, forming an ionized gas

radiation waves of energy sent out by sources of heat or light, such as the sun

radiative zone the area of the sun just outside the core, below the convective zone

solstices the days of the year with either the shortest period of daylight (the winter solstice) or the shortest period of darkness (the summer solstice)

spectroscopy the technique of observing light from an object to find out its composition, temperature, speed, or density

transit the movement of a planet or other object directly between Earth and the sun so that it can be seen from Earth as it moves across the disc of the sun

BOOKS

Barr, Catherine. *Voyage Among the Stars* (Space Voyage). Rosen Publishing Group, 2022.

Reagan, Lisa. *The Stars* (Fact Frenzy). Rosen Publishing Group, 2021.

Stratton, Connor. *The Sun* (Space). Focus Readers, 2022.

WEBSITES

Discover more about the sun at:
https://spaceplace.nasa.gov/all-about-the-sun/en

Learn more about our amazing sun at:
https://kids.britannica.com/students/article/Sun/276056

Find out more about the sun and how it influences us on Earth at:
https://www.nationalgeographic.co.uk/topic/subjects/science-and-technology/space/sun

Publisher's note to educators and parents:
All the websites featured above have been carefully reviewed to ensure that they are suitable for students. However, many websites change often, and we cannot guarantee that a site's future contents will continue to meet our high standards of educational value. Please be advised that students should be closely monitored whenever they access the Internet.

INDEX

ABOUT THE AUTHOR

Sarah Eason has written many children's books and has a particular interest in space science. She has found researching and writing this book fascinating and hopes that it helps readers better understand the mysteries of space and maybe make it their mission to become a future space explorer.